Thread of the Real

Also by Joseph Hutchison

Sentences

Greatest Hits 1970–2000

The Rain at Midnight

The Heart Inside the Heart

Bed of Coals

House of Mirrors

Sweet Nothing Noise

Wandering Music

The Undersides of Leaves

Thirst

Shadow-Light

Weathers, Vistas, Houses, Dust

Thread of the Real

Poems

Joseph Hutchison

CONUN
DRUM
PRESS

CONUNDRUM PRESS
A Division of Samizdat Publishing Group, LLC.

ISBN: 978-0-9713678-5-2

Library of Congress Cataloging-in-Publication Data is available
upon request.

Conundrum Press books may be purchased with bulk discounts
for educational, business, or sales promotional use. For
information please email: info@conundrum-press.com

Conundrum Press online: conundrum-press.com

Book Design: Sonya Unrein

Acknowledgments

The author thanks the editors of the publications in which some of these poems first appeared.

Aspen Anthology: "Complicities" (as "Henry"); *Blueroad Reader*: "Crossroads"; *The Book of George*: "Thread of the Real"; Cerise Press: "Mastery" and "Lentil Soup" [as "Sustenance"]; *Chautauqua Literary Journal*: "From a Swaying Hammock"; *Consequence Magazine*: "Field Notes Concerning the Bomb"; *Denver Syntax*: "Adrift"; *Eclipse*: "Midsummer Drought" (as "Drought in August") and "The Spring"; *Educational Insights* (ccfi.educ.ubc.ca/publication/insights): "The Glare" and "Signals"; *Evergreen Living*: "January Thaw" and "Late May on the Mountain"; *FutureCycle Poetry*: "Alba," "Days," "One Clear Moment in August" and "Yoga"; *HeartLodge*: "Kooser Creek"; *Lilliput Review*: "After Ko Un's *Flowers of a Moment*"; *Luna*: "Red Wall" and "Claritas"; *Mad Blood*: "Fox Hollow" and "Solitaire"; *Manzanita Quarterly*: "Fishing Wind River" and "A Dream of Difference"; *Midwest Quarterly*: "Open and Closed Eyes" and "Three Sentences Toward Evening After an Early Spring Storm"; *The Naugatuck Review*: "Unfinished Stories"; *The Nebraska Review*: "Winter Sunrise Outside a Café Near Butte, Montana"; *The November 3rd Club* (november3rdclub.com): "Listeners"; *Petroglyph*: "Hillside"; *Prairie Schooner*: "Mortality"; *The Rattling Wall*: "Riddles for My Father"; *Visions-International*: "Lamentation"; *Writers' Forum*: "Climbing Home at Sunset."

"George W. Bush's First Presidential Press Conference" and "George W. Bush Threatening War With Iraq" appeared in the commemorative chapbook *Poets Against the War: International Day of Protest, February 12, 2003—Evergreen, Colorado* (Mad Blood, 2003).

"Telephones" appeared in *Above Us Only Sky, Volume II* (Incarnate Muse Press, 2008).

"From a Swaying Hammock" appeared in *New Poets of the American West* (ed. Lowell Jaeger). Kalispell, MT: Many Voices Press, 2010.

Thanks to Thomas R. Smith for helping this book find its true shape.

All quotations of Heraclitus are from *Heraclitus: The Complete Philosophical Fragments*, translated by William Harris and available online at community.middlebury.edu/~harris/Philosophy/Heraclitus.html

The epigraph to "Alba" is from the poem "Joy," by Denise Levertov, from *Selected Poems of Denise Levertov*. New York: New Directions Publishing Corporation, 2003: p. 46.

The epigraph to "Telephones" is from the poem "Do Not Pick Up the Telephone," by Ted Hughes, from *Collected Poems of Ted Hughes*. New York: Farrar, Straus and Giroux, 2003: p. 585.

The epigraph to "A Dream of Difference" is from the poem "The New Colossus," by Emma Lazarus, from *Emma Lazarus: Selected Poems*, ed. John Hollander. New York: The Library of America, 2005: p. 58.

The epigraph to "Lamentation" is from the book *School of Assassins*, by Jack Nelson-Pallmeyer. Maryknoll, New York: Orbis Books, 1997: p. 19.

The epigraph to "After the Fall of Saigon, May 1975" is from *The Plague*, by Albert Camus (tr. Stuart Gilbert), in *The Plague, The Fall, Exile and the Kingdom, and Selected Essays*. New York: Everyman's Library, 2004: p. 33.

The epigraph to "Crossroads" is from "The Four Zoas: Night the Ninth," by William Blake, from *The Complete Poetry and Prose of William Blake* (ed. David V. Erdman). Berkeley and Los Angeles: University of California Press, 1981: p. 402.

Lyrics quoted toward the end of "Dark Matter" are by Tom Waits, from his song "Shiver Me Timbers," on his album *The Heart of Saturday Night*.

Two lines quoted in the "Rereading 'Hear'" subsection of "Comfort Food" are from the poem "Hear," by Lorine Niedecker, in *Collected Works of Lorine Niedecker* (ed. Jenny Penberthy). Berkeley and Los Angeles: University of California Press, 2002: p. 181.

The epigraph to "Hillside" is from the poem "Das Lied Des Idioten," by Rainer Maria Rilke, from *The Voices* (picture-poems.com/rilke/voices.html).

for Melody

Contents

I

Thread of the Real   19

Adrift   24

Climbing Home at Sunset   26

Snowstorm at Dawn   28

After Ko Un's *Flowers of a Moment*   29

On a Used First Edition of Bronk's
Manifest; And Furthermore   30

January Thaw   31

Three Sentences Toward Evening
After an Early Spring Storm   33

Kooser Creek   34

Alba   35

Open and Closed Eyes   36

II

Solitaire   41

Three Women   42

Midsummer Drought   45

Prediction   46

The Spring   47

Winter Sunrise Outside a Café
Near Butte, Montana   48

Claritas   49

Fox Hollow   50

Telephones   51

Channel One   52

III

A Dream of Difference   57

George W. Bush's First
Presidential Press Conference   58

Listeners   61

George W. Bush Threatening
   War With Iraq   62

Ambushed by a Scene on CNN   63

Opinions   64

Tests of Faith   65

Lamentation   68

After the Fall of Saigon, May 1975   69

Complicities   71

Crossroads   73

Field Notes Concerning the Bomb   75

  A Litany for the Wheeling Year   76

IV

Dark Matter   81

The Mist of Sustenance   83

Comfort Food   88

Mastery   93

The Poet's Sky (Bougnol-Quintana Hotel,
   Collioure, France: 22 February 1939)   94

V

Red Wall 99

Fishing Wind River 100

Eye Level 101

From a Swaying Hammock 103

The Glare 104

Mortality 105

Ritual 106

Late May on the Mountain 107

Yoga 108

Hillside 110

Unfinished Stories 111

Wild Irises 114

Sacred Stories 116

One Clear Moment in August 119

VI

Endnotes to a Scholarly Edition
    of an Ancient Text 123

It is in changing that things find repose.
—Heraclitus

I

Thread of the Real

*(For George, who shared the path
through the dark wood)*

Who'd have thought: setting out
from a gap in the seam
between foothills and plains,
a pinch of cocoonish
dust like me

might take wing

northwest and seaward, away
from Nixon's nightbound America
and mine,
         to settle
where vast sounds pour
their profundities into the folds
of B.C.?

Who'd have thought
I'd sleepwalk
into Canada's wooded raininess,

there to be startled awake
by a stogie-puffing

Irish Taoist?

Who was it
who'd led me to believe
there was no magic anymore?

*

He'd tap my head
like a top hat,

pull a poem
up from underneath
the false bottom—

    all ears
    and whiskery
    trepidation,
    a feeble motor
    manic in its nest
    of fur—

and pronounce it
crafty as Bugs,
or mystical-whimsical
and soft-hearted
as Harvey.

The dark
and the spotlight
and the music, he'd say,

should amaze both
audience and illusionist,

surprise even jaded
backstage crews
and fellow tricksters

with realities
fresh and unforeseen.

       *

The thread of the real
strings our words like beads

together, loops them
around our lover's neck—
they kiss her when she walks.

Or say it's a line of mindfulness
that curves between differently
grained materials, a strand
of cloudy glue squeezed clear
between inlays of rosewood
and blond bay laurel. . . .

Should the thread break,
our words will scatter, turn up
amidst ruins ages hence,
where some bemused digger
may take them for sacred—
and they were.

Hold tight, George said,
to that thread. Follow the ravel
wherever it leads. And if,
in the end, you find that it's real
only for you . . . well, then:
let that be enough.

*

Everything we cherish—

> Ovid's *Tristia*, Skelton's
> "Night Poem, Vancouver Island,"
>
> bursts of asters shadowed
> by a horizontal thrust
> of crannied arbutus trunk,

even your fearsome glimpse
of cormorant Death,
standing post above the tidal flats,
"drying its shadow on the rocks below"—

is salvage;
as when, reaching

back through calendars
unleaving like Goldengrove,

through moon-haunted mists,

through lamp-glow folding
around your writing desk,

lighting the padded yellow sheets
of paper your soft-spun voice
stitched itself across,

back through complexities
and perplexities, back
through silence,
back through gab,

I touch

a pattern
of unlooked-for
generosity,

long-gone and yet
there still, and always:

deep-hearted pagan spirit
who unbewildered
my tongue,

you taught me to live
on whatever this world
provides—no matter how
high or how low.

And once, as if we'd spent
years together, walking
the Shankill Road of your youth,
you confided, "The old Greek
had it right. The way up
and the way down—
they're the same. Y'see?
Savor the journey."

Adrift

She collapsed on the sidewalk
on the far side of the street.

He watched one passerby
pass by her . . . then another. . . .
The crowd was parting like a river.

Not that he helped her himself—
middle of a block, lunch-time
traffic risky—but later on
that day he did record it
in his journal, boiled down
to a single aphoristic sentence:

something about the indifference
of Nature . . . all of us solitary,
all of us adrift. . . .
                          Words
he can't get back (the journal
long ago lost now) now
that he could use their cold
comfort again.

                    All there is

is the image from the dream
that's shaken him awake:

the old woman's stick-legs
wrenched over the packages
she'd dropped, her wig
and gold-rimmed glasses askew,
her thick orthopedic shoes

twitching in the glare
of a gone summer, somewhere

between Fifteenth and Sixteenth
on California Street.

Climbing Home at Sunset

for Tony Barnstone
and his translations of Wang Wei

Up the steep, snow-choked
path from the failed
             car, lugging
sacks of food to the house,
the January
          dusk clawed up
a prickly glue deep
             in my chest;
and once inside, slumped
dry-mouthed in the nearest chair,
rough coughs shook
             my bones
until my tired heart knotted
(every strand of it
aching)
        and pale bruises
ghosted down the wavering
air. . . .
        Slowly, the ragged knot
loosened, and I felt
            my unmoored
gaze floating into focus on
the bookshelved walls.
             For a breath
or two I could hear the thousand
voices pouring past
            like a dismal
torrent, or the sullen blood
flooding my veins.
            Then it seemed
one voice lifted above the babble

(though Englished
out of lines
                brushed into being
ten centuries ago, in China,
in the poet's old age):
Sunset clarifies the empty river.

Snowstorm at Dawn

"It has snowed."
— *Francis Ponge,*
Memoire d'un sojourn
à les montagnes de Colorado

Dawn seems an exaggeration: there's a teeming dimness, a gloom or muffled glow alive with swirling palenesses. What light there is creeps up from the strangeness that yesterday was our valley, or down from where the sky must still arch over. Now and then, here and there, the scrappy swarm grows sparse and the southwestward ridgeline appears; gray-green smudges or brushstrokes emerge from the general effervescence . . . a feeble attempt at distinctness that's quickly overcome by freshly thickening curtains of snowfall. . . .

The flakes themselves soon become weightier. They plummet, wobbling or tumbling, through the rising brightness (we understand the sun has cleared the eastward peaks); and suddenly the storm *reacts* . . . as when passion— anger or elation, for example—begins to give way to a not-quite-calm . . . that mildly agitated exhaustion to which we so often resign ourselves, *out* of which we fashion contentment. . . .

Now the storm-cloth is growing threadbare. A blue brilliance shines through in spots, then in patches. On the opposite mountain, shadows spring from the pines until each tree stands forth in relief, edged with cold fire . . . as if engraved in gold. Soon enough we notice that the storm has unraveled into shreds of mist, a frosty raggedness adrift in the valley . . . the way the mind wanders over the floating world when there's nothing more to say.

After Ko Un's *Flowers of a Moment*

Ko Un!
I bowed to your *Flowers* each morning while shaving.
The razor's manic buzz dwindled, carried off
on the hidden waves of your breath.
From line to line I wandered, thought to thought.
A bee zapped the windowpane once, and I looked up:
mountains folding away westward under foaming clouds,
pines, crags, sun-sparks on high lakes. And then
the crazed razor shuddering in my fist,
Ko Un!

On a Used First Edition of Bronk's
Manifest; And Furthermore

The previous reader was some kind
of savage, folding a page corner down
every time a poem pleased him—two
dozen smudged dog-ears, at least.
These verses tell how nothing lasts,
and yes—I *know*. But these wrinkles
hurt. I can't seem to read until
I've uncreased each disfigured leaf,
dragging my chewed thumbnail
along the vein . . . knowing I'll never
iron it out, grinding my teeth on a curse.

January Thaw

For a moment or two,
driving through the surprise
mid-winter thaw—all
the streets sheeted
with racing melt-water,

bright ripples like the spaces
between swift lines—

Whitman, Hopkins, Clare—

the car's sun-warm
interior alive
with flickering tree-shadows—
suddenly
there

I was,
floating

above the flood
of words (language,
its abundance: available,
inexhaustible), feeling
my whole being

blossom
in the veins
of the day

as so often in my youth—the old
pulse of onwardness, of sheer

possibility . . . for just
a heartbeat or two, or three:

world without end
once again.

Three Sentences Toward Evening
After an Early Spring Storm

A bruised wind weasels off
through the long, drenched grass,
leaving as always these pools
the color of smoky quartz
where I've seen so many
faces reflected (none of them
ever quite my own)—but somehow,
their cold stares return me now
to myself at last. Beyond

the pearl bell jar of the sky,
stars continue their invisible reign
while the river, my father, groans
his gravelly blandishments
to the cloudy horizon—mother
of all my days, time keeper—
and the moon floats out of the west,
her ghostly face already turned
toward morning. Here

is my life, this roofless house—
three walls made of mist-light, one
of dusk, the floor my shadow—
and under it all a rubble mountain
startling the air with pinks of saxifrage,
mauve thistles collared in jade, tiny
milk-white flowers I used to recognize,
and will again . . . unless I invent
new names for them instead.

Kooser Creek

Despite its swiftness, the current's clear.
Grass weaves and unravels under the water.
Fish congregate among cottonwood roots
along the bank, swapping ancient tales
of Heraclitus as a boy—how he liked
to splash all alone in the murky shallows.
Out toward the middle, insect shadows
flicker over sunken plazas of sand.
How refreshing to walk there! But don't
step in unless you mean to get soaked:
the creek floor's further down than it looks.
Besides, big stones have shouldered up
here and there, sturdy enough to cross
over on. Instead, you linger. The interplay
of shade and sun-gleam's mesmerizing,
and you love how the water seems to share
the secrets you need at this very moment,
while saving the rest to tell further on.

Alba

We . . . discover ourselves
'in joy' as 'in love'.
—Denise Levertov

June dawn-light kindles
a half-dozen windows
along the street.
A breeze lifts, gentles
among the maples,

carries voices and songs
(sieved from the air
by two or three radios)
to this harbor of attention
I've anchored in. (My pen's

nib scrapes the page
like chain on a boat-rail,
and my vision
drifts). Deep shadows
spring from small things—

pebbles, forgotten toys,
newspapers—and stretch
out over grass still wet
with the glittering blood
of stars. Everything's

drenched, vivid, the whole
morning turned to a bright
pool of wax . . . the magus sun
burning it all the way back
to a tall blue candle.

Open and Closed Eyes

Lying in a windy chair in the yard, I breathe
evenly as if in sleep, but keep my eyes
wide. Birds on dark wires, roofs, clouds—
I touch them all. I breathe
and look out from my body, where the sun
has buried part of its crucial light.
I squint as the sun climbs.
Like a shovel left jammed in the mud,
I lean. I close my eyes, and the wind stills.
Fingers touch me. Grasping the handle
of my spine, they put me to use. They use me
to plant something I have no name for
(the daydream gives it no name,
though I love it). I love it and the wind
moves. I wake and breathe. I look out
at the day. I can hear leaves tossing far off
in time: the pages my bright voice will darken.
I lean toward them, listening. I keep my eyes wide.

II

Solitaire

In a crooked house, a milk-eyed crone's
turning her ragged cards. No sound

but your breathing: she feels it
as a current in the cards,

a pulse. (Who you are, she
doesn't know; and if she did,

still couldn't tell why her cards
are doors in your life.) The house—

who built it? Who granted this woman
her indifferent power? The cards

turn . . . and your breath slips
through her fingers like thread

paid out in a labyrinth:
passage on passage,

dark worlds without end.

Three Women

Healer

Her glances
pierced him, thistles

pricking the slick
hides of organs,

thorns like thermometers
testing blood. Anger

and argument—
then cold inspection.

She cut with skill, sliced
out lies like tumors;

and he recovered:
ungrateful, throat

raw with anesthesia—
the ether of scorn

she breathed
into him.

An Empty Fist

She twisted out his heart,
nailed it to a tree—this
was his dream. A long

time he stood in the dream,
watching the blood come.
Night fell . . . and when

he woke, it stayed deep
inside him somehow. Day
after day then his heart

went on like an empty fist
clenching, clenching:
nailed to a willow tree. . . .

The Ache at Midnight

Under her neck, his folded arm
had dozed off, but his heart
clattered like a castanet
in a flamenco dancer's palm:

its alacrity kept his love-worn
cock alert—made it (though
she was sleeping) nuzzle the cleft
at the root of her spine.

*

Across the candle-lit tavern table,
her love-glance. Cast so lightly,
how could she know
it would ever draw blood?

*

Some promise was made
and broken; made again, and again
broken. As if a hand held out
were hammered, hard.

Each time, desire set the bones,
and they healed; and yet
a subtle crookedness persists.
Only the ache at midnight betrays it.

Midsummer Drought

The moon dusts the leaves
of the maple with pale light,
wakes a certain woman, naked

in memory. (He feels her lift
her hips to his thirsty kiss,
in memory.) Then a bruised

cloud sails over; its massive
shadow wipes the leaves'
darkness clean. So that now

he can see, past the windowed
branches, how slowly the cloud
moves—how heavily—as if

aching with the weight
of all that rain held back.

Prediction

A breath of autumn
this late August morning—
less a chill than a weariness

in the bones. The peach tree
sags under all the fruit
it can muster, and my heart

plumps with a secret ripeness
that is sweeter than love.
Atop the elm, one yellow leaf

takes a ray of sun in hand,
burning. When it falls—
today, tomorrow—who

will notice? Just a leaf,
the first of so many small
gestures of surrender.

The Spring

Your chest's like a grave
at a crossroads, and the dead
within it shiver: their spirits
rush . . . make your backbone
bend and dip like a hazel wand.

You touched your breast, told
the curious: "Here. Sink your well
here." The timid refused. But one
labored to split you open—worked
with teeth gritted against even
your own curses—and drew up,
in the end, buckets of shadow,
nothing but shadow. . . .

Then others came, called
hopefully into your depths;
now only the echoes flow
inside you, moaning
in fear or delight—
who can say? But the ache
of that music makes you thirst,
bowing to the secret spring
you've never learned
to drink from.

Winter Sunrise Outside a Café
Near Butte, Montana

A crazed sizzle of blazing bees
in the word EAT. Beyond it,

thousands of stars have faded
like deserted flowers in the thin

light washing up in the distance,
flooding the snowy mountains

bluff by bluff. Moments later,
the sign blinks, winks dark,

and a white-aproned cook—
surfacing in the murky sheen

of the window—leans awhile
like a cut lily . . . staring out

into the famished blankness
he knows he must go home to.

Claritas

An acrid slurry creeps into the soil inside the hog farm. It soaks downward and outward, under fences, into the rain-fattened streams. From there: the rivers. . . .

Ten miles away, a boy comes home from a swim in the lake and winces drinking his milk. The first of many cankers opens its cigarette-burn between tongue and cheek.

We keep living longer, but our food lacks flavor. Our hearts flop in our chests like deformed frogs.

The President dies but continues in office.

Forgetting dreams is now habitual.

We've taken to wearing glasses that automatically darken, just to endure the sting of *claritas*.

The ozone layer thins. Days intensify. Winters strike a compromise with summers. And an acrid brightness creeps through the skin, enters the bloodstream. From there: the heart. . . .

Claritas! Your bitter truths assault us wherever we turn.

Fox Hollow

The plaque bolted to the brick gatepost
reads: FOX HOLLOW. Two-storey houses,
roofs of shake or salmon-colored tile,
throw-rug lawns, and in each garage
a cloud of gasoline fumes in the shape
of a sport utility vehicle. The streets
curve, shadowless since all the trees
are saplings, trunks taped up like legs
of halfbacks or pre-pubescent gymnasts.

We can hope that on the far side
of the enclave's wall a stubborn fox—
poised amid buffalo grass and burdocks,
amid crushed fast-food boxes—studies
the way lights toward dusk wink on
in the scattered windows. We can hope
he recalls the den of his birth, sharp
musk of his siblings, the dragging
weight of a rabbit in his jaws. . . .

Or let's admit the foxes are gone,
their hollow filled in for a playground.
Let's admit that our enclaves are named
for the absences their existence requires.
Let's ponder these sprinkler systems,
house walls painted in covenant colors,
the steel flags of street signs . . . each
one—Prairie Dog Lane, Cheyenne Circle—
raised up in memory of a slaughter.

Telephones

Sit godless when you hear
the religious wail of the telephone
—Ted Hughes

They seem to brood when the voices ignore them. As if they missed the recurring blows to the face, or—among elders of the tribe—the giddy twistings of their spirits. Over time the absence of use seems to fill them with a hunched emptiness, a lethargy . . . an oblivious slumber they now and then wake from—stammering, twittering. . . .

Hallelujah!

How they savor it: this call that arrives from beyond them and ends beyond—remote yet intimate, singular yet varied in its manifestations.

From this and ten thousand other calls like it, they've derived their ingenious religion. Someday, so the doctrine goes, a single word shall unsnarl the world's tangled circuits; redeem their personal suffering; even—who knows how?—restore their damaged bodies.

At bottom it's a simple faith. They believe that whoever made them loves them.

Channel One

At times our mind burns
like a TV turned on low
in the next room. A crow's

cackle gets through the noise,
but the hummingbird's whir's
drowned out. Why the mind

tunes in to just one channel
is a mystery. But day after day
it delivers up the same thin

shadow-dance, the same
jingles and canned laughter—
then dreams it all over all night.

III

A Dream of Difference

I lift my lamp beside the golden door!
—Emma Lazarus

The ravaged make news only in obits,
but on the front page it's all demagogues,
glassy eyed and misquoting Leviticus,
presidential committees conceived
in denial and dedicated to diversion,
polled majorities deploring condoms,
physicians who make no promises.
America discovers the source of its ills
in whatever is other and seeks to keep it
firmly there. Fags, druggies, Muslims—
let the lamp affix its sickly beam:
the American dream is a dream
of difference that protects the Good;
that is, the deserving ones: you and me.

George W. Bush's First Presidential Press Conference

February 22, 2001

1.

When asked about the bombs
lately rained down on Baghdad,
the President pinches his grin
as if toking a half-lit joint: such
hard work, choking back glee.

The aim was to send Saddam
"a clear message," he says,
then pauses, blinking. Crowds
of angels are dancing naked
on the bright pinheads
of his pupils. With a laugh
like a sleeping dog's muffled
bark in a dream, he adds:
"We got his attention."

The dead? The wounded?

Our breathless reporters press
only for bloodless numbers.

How many sorties?
How many tons of explosives?
How many "facilities" taken out?

The hypnotic calculations
of advanced technology. . . .

Logical, of course. Why inquire
after the olive-skinned natives
with their dark-age beards
and burqas, their names
that twist our tongues? Names
make rolling their deaths
into the running total
a painful exercise. And pain
impedes the pursuit of happiness.

The cameras flash and whirr;
our eyelids mimic the TV's flicker;
we succumb, nod off. . . .

2.

Asphalt lullabies beneath us
in the American dream. The car purrs
and glides; the radio anoints us
with hymns to young love, and we
sing along in our cracked falsetto.
In the American dream, music
is all road music, the road ahead
always clear. But soon
another voice rises, ghosting in
from another channel, or somewhere
off the dial. At first it's faint. *Why
are they dying?* Then stronger,
more insistent. *Because
we have so few tears falling
on our own hands.* The truth of it
showers us with cold panic. How far
are we going exactly? Who the hell
is it, driving the car—

3.

The churning
engine in our chest
startles us awake,
fingers gripping
the chair arms. Bush's
performance still burns
coolly on the tube.

Just hold on, we think. Soon
we'll be rescued by the bland
chatter of commentators,
the balm of beer ads. But now
is now: there's no escaping
the carefully mangled language
of power, the President's
unearned bravado, the press
descanting like a choir
of castratos.

Now,
looking down at our hands'
whitened knuckles,
we see that tears must bathe them
in a not-too-distant future
when our wheels go keening
down the new-laid road,
and all the maps are tattered,
and the highway signs are flying
invisibly by as we make
yet one more sentimental journey,
hurtling blindly through "the fog of war."

Listeners

October 2001

Shocked and awed, we held our tongues
those numbed weeks after the towers
crumbled. F-16s, their shuddering roar
distilled by distance into a cloudy lullaby,

claimed to speak for us—and for a time
we let them. But then their bomb bay doors
scraped open high above the old Silk Road,
over Kabul, Kandahar, Mazar-i-Sharif,

and what was made from our silence
tumbled toward lives we could almost
imagine: not ours, but like enough. Now
we ache for those stick-figures huddled

in mud-brick houses, shaken by the blasts,
pummeled by our famous skill with physics
and public relations. This ache must mean
something in us needs to speak. Listen:

the low voice, graveled by disuse, throbs
at our temples, calling up the memory
of our childhood angels—the truths
shining for us on the other side of fear.

George W. Bush Threatening
War With Iraq

The President stands at the podium
like a cobra uncoiling up from its basket.
Hooded in smugness. Eyes like beads of jet.
Now and then his tongue sips at the air,
flicking between the empty phrases.
He sways ever so slightly as he speaks,
ever so carefully, the words he did not write.
Who is it he speaks for? Who is it playing
the invisible flute only he can hear?

Ambushed by a Scene on CNN

Huddled by a bullet-pocked wall,
the burqa'd girl shelters her infant.
Behind the wall, slaughtered fighters;
slaughtered fighters in front of the wall.
A lull in the battle.

          For a moment,
nothing moves but shreds of smoke
along the shattered street—a street
named for an ancient conqueror.
A lull in history.

          We almost believe
the girl and her child will someday
breathe freely.

          Now the camera
swerves to the trees where bright
flashes of rifle fire rip the dry leaves;
bullets rip the objects of our care.
A lull in denial.

          We aim the remote,
heart-sickened by the savage
advance of our "good intentions."

Opinions

December 13, 2003

We have the tyrant in custody now—
the one who asked his staff for opinions,
then took one who spoke up next door
and put a bullet in his brain. It's true,

he poisoned whole villages—we've all
seen the pictures: bodies in the dust,
the festival of flies. In that war, though,
the tyrant was our friend, so our protest

came down to a wink, a grin. We said,
"In our opinion, you're still the big man."
Later he got out of hand, of course; seems
he never quite grasped our mission's

virtue, our love of freedom, the size
of our guns. Well, that's all done:
the tyrant's caged now, counting his lice,
crushing each one with a cracked thumbnail;

the reporters' voices stink of triumph. But
what about that boy whose arms our bombs
blew off, whose family we rubbed out: what
is *his* opinion? And what about our own

dead sons and daughters? Unlike those
who sent them to war—who stayed at home
puffing Cohibas and counting their votes—
our dead remain silent on the subject.

Tests of Faith

1

I slaughtered my first infidel,
but only after showing him
what mercy the Lord demands.
Go on, I whispered. *Say goodbye
to that wife of yours.* The man

sobbed into the hooded eye
of the camera, stammering love.
Later: two hours of fervent prayer,
five of celebration. My brothers'
cheers broke like spring rain

over my buzzing head, bathed
my fevered face. I'd begged
to be given a vision of heaven,
and had my answer: the gash
parting thick lips beneath

the gliding blade, the shudder,
the seizure of breathlessness,
the sanctified release. My hand
made rock by the strength of God.
This righteous hand!

2

I strapped my first jihadi down,
strapped down jaw and brow
to make him gape, gagged him—
then let the cold water pour. *Go on!*
I roared. *Tell us again how great*

Allah is! Hanson circled, aimed
the Handycam; the hajji thrashed,
gasped, retched—how many times?
I lost count. But, at last, he lapsed
against the board, mother-naked,

a void. *Fuck*, I said. But Hanson
had a plan. We laid the guy on ice
in a ration crate, pending the next
trash run. Later: two hours toasting
American ingenuity at the Baghdad

Country Club, 'til Hanson's head
lolled to the table. I drank on,
thanking Christ the Army drummed
every weakness out of my heart.
This well-trained heart!

3

I strangled my first poet
in the mirror. The nightmare's
pulsing alarm conjured up
a thudding 'copter, the broad
blade of its searchlight cleaving

my tongue's hoof. *The most
horrible things*, says Linh Dinh,
*become mere spectacles to the true
outsider.* Which side of my skin
is best to write on? Will I turn

into a tattoo addict, or a habitué
of opium dens? *Read an American
account of the war, and you see
how excited the writer is. He is
almost gleeful.* Linh, don't tell me

brutality's the lingua franca now!
I feel sick gutting a fish. Caught
in the gunship's shadow, I grieve
hearing news about the divorce
of Signifier and Signified.

4

I signed the executive order,
and the mosque was crushed.
I (another I) whispered a code,
and weeks later yet another I
climbed a shattered ladder

made of bomb-vest fragments
toward a hive full of virgins.
I voted billions for the Pentagon
in exchange for certain photos.
In lieu of the news, I recited

a teleprompter's lies. I marched
for peace, but no one could read
my sign's scribbled Aramaic.
My brothers and I surrounded
our whorish sister and broke her

with stones. My taxes rained
down like fire on the orphans.
Sometimes I wake in the night
and think, *The war is over.*
But another I remembers.

Note: Linh Dinh, a poet, fiction writer, essayist, translator,
anthology editor, and photographer, was born in Saigon, Vietnam,
in 1963. He immigrated to the U.S. in 1975. Quoted passages are
from Leakthina Chau-Pech Ollier's July 2000 interview with Linh;
see sonneteighteencom.blogspot.com/2007/12/interview-from-2000.
html (accessed February 17, 2012).

Lamentation

*Why has the [U.S. Army] School of
the Americas trained so many graduates
who end up being assassins, torturers,
and human rights violators?*
—Jack Nelson-Pallmeyer

Foreign jails built
of stone we quarried.
Howls of the tortured
teaching us music.

Oh listen, widows
whisper to the orphans
in our dreams. *Listen:
a heavenly choir!*

Up to our necks
in the graves
of our shadows,
singing like hell.

After the Fall of Saigon, May 1975

No doubt it was the weather.
—Albert Camus

I'd just sat back against the peeling
flagpole—a callow substitute teacher
lotteried out of the draft-board's dragnet,
lunching far as possible from the smoky
teachers' lounge—when a flurry of cries
drew my eyes from Camus's plague book
laying open on my lap. Fifty yards off,
past a screen of chainlink and flowering
crabapple boughs, a flock of white shorts
swooped low over the weedy gravel,
rubber toes clawing plumes of dust up
into the fitfully breezy air of Spring.
Ninth-grade boys. I watched them
circling a beefy ex-jarhead—the man
who'd once, earlier that school year,
glanced at my *Time* (its cover shot
of a self-immolating Buddhist monk)
and grunted, "One less gook." Now
he stood in a cyclone's eye of dogged
breath and adolescent sweat, his red
lanyard dangling a silver-bright whistle—
which he suddenly snatched up, clamped
like a shrunken skull between his lips.
A shrill, stuttering blast pierced the day.
"Pick it up, girls!" he roared. Blood
flamed into my face. With what queasy
clarity I could see my younger self
panting in that same powerless
round, goaded by the same lashes
of intimidation and awakened shame.
Just then, a big wind started to pour
down out of the distance. Blossoms flew,

and the boys sprinted through a swarm
of stinging grit toward shelter, chased
by their tormentor's barked, "Hustle up!"
The iron flagpole swayed, and I could feel
Old Glory tug as though tied to my spine.
I found it brushing the blue overhead
with a gesture both theatrical and vague,
a benediction so zealous it almost
justified all the incinerated children,
the fields sown with mines and crushed
bones, the loaded helicopters bucking
upward from our embassy roof on a wind
like this. Which wind was tearing now
at my book? Which wind made the stripes
in my country's flag crack like whips?
One wind. One wind everywhere. Wind
that finally wandered back into the distance,
letting the flag flail and slacken, letting it
fold with a weary, goodbye wave.

Complicities

*"Henry Frey was killed near Phnom Phen
last week by men under his own command."*

I was tossing old books into a box
for Goodwill when the yellowed leaf
of newsprint fluttered out, and suddenly

I was back in that sweltering August:
a kid from the block, my summer pal,
had lobbed a rock through Mr. Kilday's

bathroom window, and his old man—
wiry, flushed, lock-jawed, his cobalt eyes
pinched—came striding down the block,

blew past me in my Keds and cutoffs,
seized his son's wrist and twisted it up
behind his back. Then, with breathtaking

skill, slipped his belt off and whipped him
time after time with the buckle. "What
the hell's *wrong* with you?" he roared

between the strokes. "You little *shit!*"
Henry never cried; he barely blinked;
his clamped shut lips merely quivered.

For days crimson welts streaked his skin
like the stripes of rank he wore at the end.
I wouldn't have seen the connection then,

of course. But now it stings—recalling
how I taunted Mrs. Kilday's terrier,
wiggling my fingers through the wire

fence until he nipped a knuckle. "Fuck!"
I snapped. "I oughta *kill* that mutt."
And Henry turned . . . his cobalt eyes

bright with shared rage. "You want me
to get him tonight?" The moment blazed.
Both of us grinned when I told him yes.

Crossroads

His chains are loose his dungeon
doors are open
—William Blake

A common temptation: dig out
a clutch of coins as you idle
at the traffic light, toss it
to the shaggy derelict hunched
behind his cardboard sign, its magic
markered letters rough as runes:
HELP GOD BLESS YOU!

But think what he shelled out
for that cigarette, whose smoke
creeps up through his beard's
tangle. What must that draggled
mutt of his cost to feed? And there,
where his camouflage jacket pocket's
ripped—isn't that the grimy cap
of a pint poking up?

At last the light blinks green,
the traffic surges. Saved again
by the computerized rhythm
of rush hour! Your stomach
soothed by the savage verdicts
of Herbert Spencer. . . .

Then tire-shrieks and a bash
and hail of glass up ahead
make you brake, make blood
stumble in your chest—and you're
stuck again, stranded at the crossroads.
Where are the sirens? Where the law?

There's only the beggar's stare,
unwavering. And so you turn,
then can't turn away. Those eyes
burning in their nest of thorns—
you've seen that look of transport
before: years ago, in a dream.

The child in your dream
had a father who kept a dwarf
bound in the cellar. Nine nights
the boy kept searching, until
he found where the key lay hidden,
and took it, and crept downstairs,
and set the little prisoner free.
How the boy's eyes shone
as you plunged into the forest!
A full moon sailed high up
on waves of tangled branches,
its silver blood lighting
your lucky way. . . .

Small wonder you ache
to tramp the gas pedal down.
But trapped as you are, instead
you let your hand burrow
into your pocket, let it
root for change—the dull coins
chiming like links of a broken chain.

Field Notes Concerning the Bomb

The bald, jug-eared foreign policy expert advocates bombing Tehran.
The ex-Director of Mossad wants to bomb Beirut or Damascus, or both.
The CEO of Raytheon aims to grow the lucrative cluster bomb market.

*

The audience enjoys hooting and jeering when the stand-up comic bombs.
The gamer whoops when the dusky bomber explodes in a cloud of red pixels.
When Wile E. Coyote gets bombed to ash, the toddler cries, "Beep beep!"

*

The Sudanese med student wants to bomb the arrogant Danish cartoonist.
The talk radio fanatic suspects his neighbor's gardener of planting a bomb.
The born-again President dreams of cramming a bomb up the Devil's ass.

*

The émigré poet begs Jesus to bomb the dictator who raped her voice.
The pilot bombs a mud-brick hovel, then flies off above the ascending dust.
Glimpsing himself in a lobby mirror, the Jakarta Hilton bomber hesitates.

*

Its builders, dealers, devotees and victims mean nothing to the bomb.
The bomb needs nothing and desires nothing—not even to explode.
Anti-Buddhas: each bomb's awakening makes even emptiness suffer.

A Litany for the Wheeling Year

with apologies to Thomas Nashe

Again a grim old year is turning.
Again the fires of war are burning.
Again the poor cough up their lives.
Again rich men adorn their wives.
The moon's balsamic, a sleepy eye.
We stare sullenly up and sigh.
    Who'll have mercy on us?

Not the CEO of Goldman.
Not the gangsters in the Forum.
Not the grinning, bailed-out bankers.
Not the pundits hyping rancor.
The moon declines toward total night.
We switch the late news on and sigh.
    Who'll be honest with us?

Look at how our God-dreams kill us.
Look at how our wills are will-less.
Look at how we've too much fondness
For the blood-dimmed tide that haunts us.
The moon has sailed off down the sky.
Our hearts go darker as she flies.
    Who'll help us escape us?

Now the Times Square angel's falling.
Now the crowds below are squalling.
Drums are throbbing, horns are braying.
Sometimes going feels like staying.
Two . . . One . . . A blast of white.
We stare into the heart of light.
    Another year's upon us.

IV

Dark Matter

for Tom Auer,
in memoriam

On my way to your wake, stuck at a stoplight,
this talk radio voice drifts out of the ether—
some cosmologist, keen on deep space:

> *The Hubble telescope's found light*
> *in just four percent of the universe.*
> *The rest is full of something we call*
> *"dark matter."*

Odd, how the notion relaxes my knotted throat.
Everything must go! Cities. Farms. Nations.
Earth itself will be slag—a frozen tear. . . .

The light blinks green and I stamp the gas.
Across town your friends are gathering now,
bringing stories about your love of books
and your daily kindness. Among the heartfelt
bromides, the helpless shrugs and far-off stares,
I'll know your erasure's just a red-shift blur,
your life—like all lives—a stray particle
sparked off by the night machine. . . .

For a mile or more it seems almost all right,
until the station veers from talk to music—
piano waves and a salt-scarred voice:

> *I'm leavin' my fam'ly,*
> *leavin' all my friends.*
> *My body's at home*
> *but my heart's in the wind. . .*

Rolling blues that would make you sway.
Would have made, I mean. Just months ago.
Back when it seemed we had nothing but light.

The Mist of Sustenance

Lost Time

At the end of our last visit, I waved
as the car slowed away from the curb,

and Dad waved back—straightened
in his wheelchair where he'd parked it
at the living room's picture window,

and raised both arms and moved them
like a signalman wielding invisible flags
on a ship's sinking deck. With a shock

I saw that he was waving to a vanishing
image of himself, signaling in distress,

at sea in a mirror made of lost time.

*

Days

The backs of my father's hands,
splashed with bruises . . . the dream
had scrubbed them clean. His heart
was healed, and the raw gravel
grinding down his knee joints
had been washed away. I thought
that for the first time in years
his ears could catch sparrow song,
chitter of squirrels, faint breath
of a breeze in the shadowy trees
around his garden. I saw him crouch
to test a tomato's redness, then stand
up easily, giving it a few days more.

Months later that simple image
can sting my eyes until they glisten,
seeing how the dream had granted him
days without end.

*

Riddles for My Father

> *Whatever we see when awake is death;*
> *when asleep, dreams.*
> —Heraclitus

He began in Colorado.
Anyplace he loved was home.
His breath scarred by cigarettes
was a rough-barked branch;
an orphaned owl hunched there,
amber eyes cradling a banked fire.

The moon was new all of his life.
The stars trafficked in secrets.

Only the earth woke in his hands
that were strong as barn-door hinges,
and he savored the give and take
of seed and harvest. His nightmare:
an upright pitchfork forgotten
deep in a mound of hay.

But always there was a horse
snorting in its damp stall,
and a saddle on the stall rail,
and not far off some mountains,
and canyons a man might live
another life in, and rivers he might
step into and out of at will. . . .

(He'd never have heard Heraclitus
in those lines, for who in our family
would have loved such riddles
but me? I knew he'd declare them
dark and not to be trusted—so
I always held my tongue.)

Now he sleeps in the earth,
in that long dreamless house
clods drummed down on
like hooves. His face
is a new moon, and all
that was starry in him flies
like a dry beam of light
away from me. His hands
lay like broken sheaves
at his sides.

I'm awake.
And Heraclitus
is ashes in my mouth.

*

Cloudy Night Window

The mound of lentils, freshly washed, dripped in a gray
aluminum colander in the sink while his father did magic
with the stock-pot: bouillon cubes, barley, carrots, crescent-
moons of celery, fat tomato chunks, the translucent petals
of yellow onion, the rich mystery of spices. Above the
sink, elm branches crazed the west-facing window, sifted
the bleak last light as it drained away beyond the broken
wall of peaks. February? Early March? Still winter for sure.
(It's winter where his father's grave steeps in the rain of
other mountains, in a future that is now and yet seemed so
remote then—impossible, in fact.) He lifted the colander

and shook the lentils into the pot, quelling its boil, then stirred and stirred with a long wooden spoon until the broth was roiling again. He turned the burner knob to low and laid the lid in place. Soon enough they'd all sit down at the blue Formica table, the bowls and spoons already set out, and breathe in the earthy steam. The night window would be cloudy then, thick with the mist of sustenance that hid the darkness from them.

*

A Celebration

The revolving door gasped
behind me, and I drifted onward
into the room: the carpet plush,
a ceiling lost in vaulted shadows.
On the far wall a milky glow
poured through high windows.
The celebration was in my honor,
but I wished I wasn't there—all
the faces vague, the hubbub
churning. In an open sitting area
(sofa, chairs, the table-lamps dim)
Mom stood, clutching her purse,
eyes alive with coy mischief,
her smile haunting as a fox's.
Before I could speak she glanced
off to her right, and I saw him—
taller than me for the first time
in thirty years. His changed skin
shone like moon-washed snow,
his hair grown thicker and white
as apple blossoms. I thought
to ask him how he'd come there,
but suddenly he was cloaked

in a cloudy light. In silence
I stepped toward him, a calm
overtaking me like those summer
dawns we'd crawl from our tent
to fish Jakey's Creek, a barren mile
from where it eased into the cold
Wind River. The closer I came,
the more Dad loomed. Reaching
up, I slipped my arms around
his waist and touched my cheek
to his stomach's warmth. He said
nothing, but cupped his hands
lightly over my shuddering
shoulder blades, as if gentling
a horse—and I clung to him.
Against my will I clung to him,
as he could no longer cling to me.

Comfort Food

Long Distance

His mother knows
who but not where
he is. She warns
into the phone, "Don't
rake leaves too long,
you'll hurt your back."
Out his window,
leafless piney ridges,
the farther ranges
snowbound. "Don't
worry now," he says.
"I'll be careful."

Next time she knows
where but not who.
"You never *listened*,"
in a child's voice.
"It's me," he begins.
She snaps: "You think
I don't *know* that?"
And suddenly she's
chatting about the rain
and fog out her window,
there at the far other
end of the line.

*

Breath

The world enters
us as breath. We

return it to itself
as breath. When

we're done with
the world, where

(he wonders) does
all that breath go?

*

A Travelin' Woman

The last words his mother said to him
were (as usual) long distance. Freed
at last from the doctors' clutches,

delivered by wheelchair into the human
tenderness of hospice, she exulted
into the phone: "I'm a travelin' woman!"

"Where you headed?" he said, buoyed
by her joy. "Where?" she laughed.
"I don't know. Timbuktu!"

*

Dream Image After
the First Good Cry

westwarding river—
red-gold shreds of Sun scattered
on it and in it

★

Open Casket

She's a stranger, though he has to agree

they've done a beautiful job with her hair,
and yes she looks peaceful, out of pain,

and the silk blouse under the black sweater
shines like the petals of a sun-struck lily,
and the hands, one atop the other, look

as if he'd held them. Knowing he doesn't
know this stranger, though, he turns away,

eyes shut tight to remember his mother.

★

Going On

They knew her breath would stop,
as her husband's breath had stopped.
As people by the thousands every day
stop, breathing the world back one

last time into itself. Like all mourners,
they felt the world itself should stop.

But no. The world simply took her
last breath back—then began to share

it among them in the form of weeping.
Like a sacred bread. This sorrow bread.
Can this be the secret, then? The breath
they all had shared with her so long

still here, in the world—the world's
going-on keeping it in circulation?
Small wonder they savor the ache of it:
the unstopped breath of a mother's love.

★

Rereading "Hear"

after Lorine Niedecker

Twenty-some years
back he sounded out
her transcription of
mourning doves

               You

ah you

        her mother
gone gravely still

Only now has he
come to hear those
doves her way:

              True

too true

        he longs
to say—

To whom?

*

Comfort Food

A fifty-something crying in the dairy aisle,
lost in a dream of his dead mother. Grief
welled up in him, "out of nowhere"
(as they say), and now he's a spectacle.

At least his display turns out to be brief.

He smiles abjectly a moment, "gathers
his wits," lets loose a broken sigh—
then picks out the goods he came to buy.
Butter. Cheese. The whole milk of childhood.

Mastery

Then shall the lame man leap as a hart,
and the tongue of the dumb shall be free.
—Isaiah 35:6

Across the steep field, amid grasses
twitching like blown tatters of bandage,

I saw Paul Celan *dalag*—hazarding a dance,

albeit weighted down by an ashen overcoat
so that his dance seemed a sort of stagger,

anguished, euphoric, exacting, adroit—as if

this halting mastery might distract or scare off
the hound of oblivion snapping at his heels.

The Poet's Sky
(Bougnol-Quintana Hotel, Collioure, France: 22 February 1939)

These blue days and this sunshine of childhood . . .
—Antonio Machado

The poet could only flee this far.
Between his deathbed and the agony
of his homeland—mountains, bleak
canyons, wind-battered crags. It seems
someone's hacked off his gouty legs
and wrapped them in that slick paper
he often, as a boy, fetched shanks
of lamb in for his mother; it seems
someone's dumped them in a rough
gully: they twitch like two hurt animals
snarled in brambles. No going on now,

the fever says—but won't tell him if
the *words* will go on, the clear words
from the fountains of his youth, words
from Soria's arid plains, where his first
and last love, Leonor, lies buried. He
squints to see them, the words, floating
just above his slack, cracked mouth
like rainbowed soap bubbles, or a haze
of flies dancing in tight satin jackets.
They've come this far to find him.
Now some honeyed coolness pours

down all his length, and his gaze
strays to the window, its snow-washed
cloudless sky—not Spanish, not French:
his own. He twists up onto one elbow
and fishes among pill bottles and glasses
on the bedside table for his stub pencil

and the only paper—a sweat-stained
railway schedule. With aching fingers,
he ekes out in the margin a last first line:
Estos días azules y este sol de infancia.
In cold exile, an invincible summer.

V

Red Wall

They say there were orchards and truck farms a few miles away. I remember bushel baskets made of thin wooden slats wired together, with handles also of wire, tipped forward at a whitewashed roadside stand Dad had driven us to in the pale green Plymouth from the house on Elm Court. But mainly it's the house I recall, and the yard. Raspberry hedges gripped the back fence; on the north side a cherry tree, dark-leafed, the cracked bark dusky, the fruit almost black—like a puncture wound—and very sweet; and in the center a huge Dutch elm. Snow-on-the-mountain and clusters of hens-and-chicks hugged the ground between the sidewalk and the one-car garage. In a dream the basement stairway went up instead of down from the kitchen, dead-ending at the ceiling, and a severed hand lay on it halfway up (no blood anywhere): I dreamed this many times and always woke in a choking panic. . . .

What all these memories mean, I don't know. And what about the images I've remembered wrongly? The thousands simply forgotten?

Maybe the mystery isn't that this or that happened, but that any of it existed at all. That I was there or seemed to be there, and am there no longer—though sometimes it seems I still am. There. As though it all exists, unchanged somewhere. Untouched beyond a red wall of years.

Fishing Wind River

Hip-deep in water and drowned in the roar,
I stood fast sailing backward, dared not
close my eyes for fear of toppling
into the thrilling wrestle of the current.
I was fishing like my father, who hugged
the upstream bank where willows hung
sways of shadowy hair around him;
shadowy his form as he cast the worm
far, into the stillest pools. . . .

Years ago . . . and yet some days,
even now, that flashing current surges
in a minute or a second to my waist
and hugs like a lover. "Get over
to the bank!" I hear my father yell.
"Do you *want* to be swept away?"
My good father—a shade in shadows,
shouting his warning from the shallows,
poised between the willows and the Wind.

Eye Level

The hawk hangs
in hard wind
twenty yards out
from the bedroom
window, spread
feathers thrashing
in the bluster.

A gale
as when grief
pours down
off jagged peaks,
punishing as it
strangely
lifts us. Or
when we float
above the green
world, avid
for a glimpse
of quickness in
the seething
grass, a morsel
of breath that might
stay our craving.

The hawk
(hanging there
at eye level,
swaying beyond
reach) flashes
one keen
glance—and I
can't help but look
and look away.

Whether or not
it sees me, I don't
pretend to know.

From a Swaying Hammock

With a raw squawk the raven breaks
his glide and alights on a pine's

spring-like branch. What peaks gleam
in his onyx eye? What fat anoints his beak?

When I doze, it seems I hear my name
picked apart by his artful caws,

feel the combs of his claws
prowling among my graying hairs.

How can I sleep with him perched there?

The Glare

This slug on the path is both slick and slow-witted. They usually stick to the granite coolnesses in the rock garden, but this fellow's managed to wander into the sun's killing glare. Maybe the morning's overcast made him think *dusk*, and venture out. Anyway, now he races—there is no other way to say it—"sluggishly" toward the lilac-shadowed grass. Not blindly, though. As we bend down to study him, the creature curls upward, waving his antennas like little drunken fists. Then he goes back to hauling an invisible heaviness across the warm flagstone. It must be that his mortality weighs as much as ours, because we're drawn to his ache, his speechless effort . . . watching him arch and stretch like the tongue in a dying man's mouth. . . .

Mortality

Hard to imagine yourself
in the ground . . . a shabby mess
of broken spindles, the loom
that cranked out the cloth of you
smashed, scattered—and somewhere
the ego sputtering its rage.

You can hear it now—railing
like a mill-town dowager
piqued, let's say, by the country's
fraying moral fiber. Her spotted fist
gavels the tea-table, making
the bone teacups clatter.

"Oh! The very idea!"

Ritual

Meloxicam to soothe the angry disk between L2 and L3, pinched and bulging like a bitten tongue. Prilosec to save the stomach from the ravages of Meloxicam and to keep down the Resveratrol (an oblong lump of compressed soot said to keep the blood vessels pliant and cancer at bay). Also a capsule of fish oil the warm color of tequila *añejo*, and vitamin C of course, and a packeted pile called Nature's Code whose purpose I can't recall. Nevertheless I wash the whole handful down every morning with a half-sweet, half-biting antioxidant berry-juice mixture made to scrape chemical rust off the walls of my many millions of aging cells. As in the past, in eras rife with superstition—irrational, unscientific, fearful of demons, djinns, ghosts of ancestors, rival gods: this irritable reaching after time and health, this hapless genuflection to the Invisible.

Late May on the Mountain

Strong wind bends the poplar almost flat;
its tough leaves thrash in a fine, green frenzy.
It's like some preacher seized by the Spirit,
shouting holy gibberish.
                              And the congregation
answers: a seethe of hillside grass, pansies
flaunting colors like a Pollack come alive,
even the stiff-backed ponderosas sway—all
aching to be *swept away*.
                              Their roots, though,
know something deeper: they grip down,
holding on even harder to *this* world.

Yoga

for Melody

The teacher guides their breath
into a depth his doesn't like
at first. He lets her make
his lungs plump up, then

lead his body into Downward
Facing Dog. The class has seen
what her body does; but his—his
just isn't made the same. Her glance

argues, *All you lack is discipline.*
Why? Those years in school,
outwitting bullies, making grades,
escaping into books—didn't his body

bear him like a mule on its back?
Suddenly, tremors invade his arms—
but the teacher's fierce. "Hold it. Hold it."
He breathes into his shaky limbs

because she says he can . . . breathes
(it hits him) because *she* breathes
so beautifully. It must be *her*
he wants to breathe in! "Good,"

she announces. "Child's Pose."
He collapses with the rest, folded
around his secret. Or do the others
sense how intently he listens

as her naked feet brush the bare
wood floor? Now she halts, inches
from his tucked head. "Just relax,"
she says. And he tries. He tries!

"And don't forget to breathe."

Hillside

"Wie gut."
— Rilke

Blond grasses furred with afternoon light,
like a crowd of people suddenly seized

by one thought. The same light woos
darkness from slender pine-bodies,

whets the sword-edge of a cloud.
A breath of wind touches the hollow

between our shoulder blades. How good.
What waits for all will wait a while longer.

Unfinished Stories

for Shannon

Nine may be too old for this,
my wife's look suggests.
My eyebrows crumple.
Really? Nine's too old?

Let's see.

We snuggle her between us
like when she was seven,
plump the pillows behind us,
pull the covers up under our chins.

"A peanut-butter-and-jelly sandwich
was walking through the forest..."

We take turns inventing
its sandwichy adventures.
It can eat and be eaten,
be squashed by an elephant,
marry a telephone or a dill pickle,
play the trombone at a monkey party.

(Mention of monkeys
gives us permission to jut
our jaws and puff out
our cheeks,
scratching and grunting,
screeching like crazed violins.)

Sometimes we wander off
with a skunk or a tightrope walker
and forget where we left the sandwich.
Poor sandwich! Its peanut butter

melting in the broiling sun
by an empty highway in Arizona,
strawberry jelly leaking from the crust
where it scraped against a cactus. . . .

We pass the story around
a good long while sometimes.
Sometimes just a turn or two
brings us to the end.

"The end!" she announces,
and we send the sandwich off
on another adventure. Or she says,
"I'm tired," and my wife says,
"Go get in your bed."

Tonight it's tiredness.
We leave the sandwich
under a striped umbrella
on a Mexican beach.

I get a kiss, as always,
but Gramma tucks her in
and rubs her back. Soon
her breathing relaxes;
her face grows soft as a rose.

My wife crawls back in bed,
and we lay awake awhile.

The story still glows in our heads,
but it casts a few shadows too.
Some not too distant day
she'll say, "Oh Gramma, Grampa—
let's not tell that silly story!"

After that our sandwich
will have no more adventures.
It will vanish in the underworld
of unfinished stories. . . .

A world
very much like this one.

Wild Irises

for Melody, again

Half asleep in the half-empty bed,
I touched your absence as I did
those ancient, troubled months
when I couldn't trust you'd ever
lie by me again—then lapsed

toward the dream that ached
like a hiding child's held breath.
Night. A lake. Restless winds.
The cloud-swaddled moon broke
through here and there, chalked

fragmentary ciphers on the ripples.
The scene like something turned up
in Tarot: a cloak-bowed wanderer,
his path pinched between dark water
and darker woods. Then a sudden

shift of cloud: brightness streams
from the moon's jade jar; the cloak
weighs my own shoulders down.
At my feet, wild irises—hundreds
swaying near and far in the radiance,

their open petals thin as the veil
between this life and the next,
their scent your scent, their leaves
tracings of your body's curves. How
is it, I wonder, that I ever feel lost

when your beauty lies all around me?
And then I start off, down the path,
like a fresh line of verse—drawn
onward by onwardness, toward some
kind of waking, some end without end.

Sacred Stories

Breezy golden light
on the mountain.
Breath by breath,

you climb the rope
of listening and vision
down into the valley,

where the pine-tree
people have already
slipped into a tall,

swaying sleep, while
(in their slim shadows)
the grass people lean,

whispering their most
sacred story: how bleak
this valley was before

their ancestors sailed
an ocean of wind
into its barren folds.

*

Your ancestors came
from Germany via Ukraine,
from Ireland and Scotland.
Dirt farmers, mostly,

mostly half-assed about it,
buying rocky ground (sight
unseen, but cheap), then
trundling west in Conestogas,

iron-jawed women birthing
and burying along the trail.
Wherever they settled, they'd
one day head to town and glare

into a lens for a family portrait.
What can you buy with joy,
their lampblack eyes would ask,
on this enemy Earth?

*

Here where Arapaho and Ute
hunted deer in summer, cut poles
for tents, told sacred stories—here
your people platted cramped parcels,
hammered cabins out of scabrous

pine logs, so that moneyed types
could flee the flatland swelter
and odious foreign laborers. Then:
1929. At big desks of burnished oak,
ruined men pressed pistol barrels

to their heads, leaving only a stench
of saltpeter and scorched pomade.
Soon the elite sanctuary's gates
were flung wide to almost anyone
with cash. If not for those shattered

Easy Street fortunes, there'd be no
you pondering these pines, that grass,
that ginger-furred fox, that Taoist
flash of a magpie into the leafy brush.
Why this melancholy, then? You grasp

the meaning of your past, the present
with its evening sun bleeding down
beyond the ridge. No stories here
mention you. But true to your class,
you keep on dreaming of being *let in*.

One Clear Moment in August

When I let the long snake
of water in the garden hose
out into the garden, sun
sparkled along its sleek length.
How it split, multiplied, flashed
down the rows of ripe corn—
like desire that ripples
among beautiful women,
or some promise that threads
the dreams of sleepers, linking
scattered towns. So the water
snake touched onion greens
and pepper stalks, carrot-leaf
sprays, thick bursts of broccoli,
muttering to the roots: *Here I am,
as always, to give you strength.
There is nothing to fear.
This kiss is forever.*

VI

Endnotes to a Scholarly Edition
of an Ancient Text

1. The text here is corrupt and more than usually tantalizing.
2. A reference, perhaps, to unguents that were widely reputed to prolong sexual pleasure.
3. A kind of tamarind. Its bark was powdered and used to spice the sacramental wine.
4. Another corruption. Bausch proposes "toenail"; Klein, with typical audacity, suggests "nipple."
5. A perfumed scarf laid over the dead person's face, through which loved ones would kiss the corpse's mouth. Evidently an allusion to their proverb: "Last breath, sweetest breath."
6. A startling example of what Kronstadt calls "their dark humor, which flashes like shards of obsidian in moonlight."
7. The ambiguous compound verb encourages some confusion as to whether the wife or the lover is being addressed; this may be intentional. Klein points out that this verb form in other surviving texts is used exclusively in reference to deities.
8. Another unguent, possibly derived from aloe and used to mitigate the effects of overzealous fellatio.
9. A constellation so vast that no earthbound observer can see it whole. Kronstadt views this as evidence of seafaring; Bausch believes the description was pieced together from second-hand accounts.
10. A honey cake made from barley husks and thorns. Called, perhaps ironically, "Traveler's Delight."
11. Kronstadt: "Clearly a hoopoe"; Bausch: "A sparrow"; Klein: "A miniature peacock." Its perch "high upon her inner thigh" leads me to believe we're presented with a metaphorical bird—in reality a deliciously placed birthmark. This explains the evident pleasure our

author takes in its "subtle fluttering."

12. What I translate as "a broken flute" Klein risibly renders as "a bent Pan pipe."

13. To Kronstadt this apparent stammering suggests glossolalia; Bausch has proposed an affliction such as epilepsy. Klein, unsurprisingly, reads stammered passion here. My solution is meant to suggest all three.

14. The metaphor seems to hint at a quality of waywardness in the River of Heaven.

15. The climax has not survived—erased by fire from the Cologne Codex, by insect activity from the fragments found at Narbonne. The absence of our story's ending has broken many a scholar's heart. Mine is no exception.

CPSIA information can be obtained at www.ICGtesting.com
Printed in the USA
BVOW03s1444070415

395095BV00004B/172/P